Praise for Quiet Time

"Every mom needs time to step back, unwind and, most importantly, connect with God. If you are looking for a respite from being overwhelmed by the busy mom life, I highly recommend Quiet Time!"

—**Ruth Schwenk**, founder of **The Better Mom**,
co-author of *For Better or For Kids*
and *Pressing Pause*

"Oh weary mama, I've been there (& I am there). This parenting gig is rough. Guilt over angry outbursts and exhaustion from endless needs, we end the day feeling pretty beat up. Thankfully, Samantha offers understanding and encouragement through her relatable stories and Biblical wisdom. Quiet Time ministered to my soul after a long day ministering to little souls. May these pages provide nourishment and filling so you can pour out to your little people today."

—**Heather MacFadyen**,
founder of **God Centered Mom**

"I thoroughly enjoyed my journey through this Devotional Retreat. Practical and honest, I saw the dailyness of my own beautiful/messy life in its pages. Samantha points back to Christ at every turn and clearly is a mom struggling well."

—**Emily Thomas,**
founder of **Mom Struggling Well**

"I first caught the fresh perspective of Samantha's writing when we worked together at RightNow Media. And I admired her commitment when she left to stay at home with her growing family. I'm happy I still can enjoy her godly insight and find myself gently challenged by her words."

—**Jackie Mosley**,
senior publisher, **RightNow Media**

"As a fellow mom in the trenches, I can say wholeheartedly that Samantha Krieger's devotional Quiet Time speaks to me right where I live. With compassion, grace, and real-life experience, Samantha encourages mothers in their faith, their friendships, and navigating the ins and outs of mothering. Reading this book is like having a coffee date with one of your best friends; you'll come away refreshed."

—**Brandy Bruce**, author of Looks Like Love
and the Romano Family series

Quiet Time

A 30-Day Devotional Retreat
for Moms in the Trenches

Blessings to you,
Samantha xoxo

BY SAMANTHA KRIEGER

ACKNOWLEDGEMENTS

My husband, Jeremiah—for your love, leadership, and shepherd's heart. You're the rock of our home and the man I'm proud to call my own. Your suggestions and theological insight have made this book what it is. I love you.

My children, John, Rebekah, Hannah & Will—for giving me the majority of these stories and being my constant inspiration. I love being your Mommy.

My parents, Dennis & Becky Edwards—your generosity, support, and sacrificial love all these years have marked me eternally and I am forever grateful for you.

Megan Bates, New Leaf Creative Studio—for your talented design and putting a vision into a beautiful reality.

Elizabeth Vanwingerden—for the gorgeous hand-lettered bible verses throughout.

Jean Clayton—your encouragement and humor in the editing process kept me persevering.

Carol Cool—for your excellent communication, copy editing skills, and attention to detail.

MOPS (Mother's of Preschoolers) Lakeside Baptist Church, Dallas, Texas—you were my lifeline, community, and safe haven as a new mom.

Todd Wagner, Pastor, Watermark Community Church, Dallas, Texas—for many years of solid and practical preaching.

First Baptist Church, Holyoke, Colorado, Mom's Bible Study—for your encouragement, laughter, and support. Tuesday mornings are better because of you.

Thank you.

CONTENTS

$\mathcal{P}art\ One$

Finding Your Calm in Christ

Part Two

Quieted by His Love

INTRODUCTION

Refreshing Waters
for Your Weary Soul

A few months ago, for the first time since having kids, I escaped from my home and met three of my close girlfriends—Julia, Jen, and Ashley—for a weekend getaway in Berthoud, Colorado—a rural town backdropped with green pastures, a glistening river, and snow-capped mountains. We've known each other since we were newlyweds and grew closer after the births of our babies. We have fifteen kids among us, and Julia and Ashley are still having them!

Our time away was a much-needed retreat from the chaos, noise, neediness, and daily demands in our homes. We enjoyed dining out and walking, and we spoiled ourselves with late-night movies, half-priced Frappuccinos, and a spa day. I can still smell the Aveda eucalyptus oil from our heavenly facials. We even got caught in a thunderstorm while shopping and laughed as we ran back to Jen's van, all soaking wet. Thankfully, she's the prepared one and had rain jackets packed in her trunk.

Withdrawing from my familiar world renewed my strength and helped me become a better wife, mom, and friend. The quiet time away from the clatter helped me refocus and be reminded of God's plans for me, my husband, and my children. And reconnecting with women who know me best spurred me on to persevere through the difficult days.

My prayer is that this devotional book will touch you in the same way—like refreshing waters for your soul, strengthening you in the sweet and sacrificial work of motherhood. Wherever you are in your journey, I'll bet we can share similar stories together and some tears too.

My years in motherhood have been eventful to say the least— seven emergency room visits, all kinds of bodily fluids to clean up, emotional highs and lows, fights to break up, food complaints, school adjustments, multiple meltdowns, attitude problems, permanent marker all over the kitchen table (thanks, Melaleuca oil, for erasing the creativity), unexpected hospital stays, "Mom, I hate you" moments, "Mom, I love you" epiphanies, and many more.

Recently, our mail carrier said my three-year-old son met her buck-naked in his rain boots at our mailbox—smiling with his big chocolate-brown eyes. She wondered where I was. I'd no idea he escaped out the front door in just a matter of seconds.

Let's just say I'm learning not to worry too much about what people think, to laugh a little more, and to thank God for watching over my kids when apparently I can't!

I write as a fellow mom and friend smack-dab in the trenches with you. Every day I'm learning about my desperate need for Jesus and his relentless grace. I fail and fall often, but at the end of the day it's always Jesus who rescues me and picks me back up. In him, I'm able to find my rest and hope when I can't seem to find it anywhere else.

As you read each day's entry, I pray you'll find a sense of calm and, most importantly, see you're not battling the challenges of motherhood alone. I pray you'll grow closer to Jesus and feel better equipped and encouraged in who you are in Christ, what you're doing in the daily grind, and where God has placed you in this sacred season of your life as *Mommy*.

Thank you so much for reading. I'm cheering you on.

—*Samantha*

Part One

Finding Your Calm in Christ

FOR I WILL *Satisfy* THE WEARY *Soul*

JEREMIAH 31:25

DAY 1

Pinterest and the Potter

"But now, O Lord, you are our Father;
we are the clay, and you are our potter;
we are all the work of your hand."
Isaiah 64:8

M y friend Katie is one of the most gifted people I know. She started her own Etsy shop that's grown to be highly successful, she's a talented photographer who's gifted in all things do-it-yourself, and her entire home looks like a Pinterest explosion. To top it off, she has three strikingly adorable kids and a hardworking husband.

One day over coffee we got on the topic of comparing ourselves to our friends on Facebook and Instagram and how sometimes we feel as if we just don't measure up. I told her how I'd even compared myself to her. Then she surprised me: "I've thought less of myself when seeing *your* gifts too!"

We laughed and talked about how there are two sides to every story. Social media is typically filled with the sweet spots of life—rarely the struggles and pains—seldom the yelling-at-your-children, no-makeup, and unshaved-legs kind of days. News feeds can make it difficult not to wish you were someone or somewhere else. It's tough to remember God has good plans for us when we're so busy watching the life that's being flawlessly fleshed out in others.

God's Word reminds us we're all the work of his hands.

God's Word reminds us we're all the work of his hands. He's fashioned and shaped us for his purposes, all of which are different and unique. Make no mistake: The hands of your potter are perfect. You can trust his loving hands that not only created you but also are showing you his plan and will for your life.

God's desire is for us, the clay, to be wholly his so he can shape us as he wills. He knows how stubborn we are, yet he is patient with us as our heavenly Father. We discover his will not by looking at what others are doing or even within ourselves but by looking to Christ alone.

When you're tempted to measure your stature, newsfeed, or highlight reels against another's, remember to fix your gaze on the potter—whose hands are gently holding you and making you into his beautiful and desirable image. It's in him where you'll find all the joy, satisfaction, purpose, and understanding in who he made you to be and what he's called you to do.

When you submit to his sovereignty in your life—in how he distinctively created your personality, passions, gifts, talents, and abilities—you'll unmistakably find your calling and contentment.

Thank God today for the talents he's entrusted you with for his glory. Chances are good someone needs you today—*exactly* for who you are.

Prayer

> Jesus, sometimes I feel so weak and my heart wanders toward the glorious works of others rather than reveling in your handcrafted work of intentionally and beautifully creating me. I confess my ever-present struggle with envy, jealousy, and covetousness. Help me to trust your plan for my life, and give me the grace to measure myself against your standard alone. Amen.

DAY 2

Rivers in the Desert

"Behold, I am doing a new thing;
now it springs forth, do you not perceive it?
I will make a way in the wilderness
and rivers in the desert."
Isaiah 43:19

My husband and I were living in a tiny two-bedroom, one-bathroom apartment in seminary housing with our newborn daughter and two-year-old son. A major construction project was being done on our building—a complete resurfacing of the bricks. Constant banging, drilling, scraping, and pounding shook our walls, and a blue tarp covered our window for more than five months.

As if that wasn't enough, I was also sleep deprived, managing our home and the needs of my children, while my husband was working full-time and going to school. I could feel my emotions and anger welling up. After I washed the dishes, I grabbed the tray off the high chair and slammed it on the countertop. All the noodles and sauce went flying, and a plastic piece broke off the tray. My son looked terrified—what was happening to Mommy?

Guilt and shame flooded my soul; I couldn't get his frightened expression out of my mind. *I need help, God*, I cried. *Save me.* I was stuck at the bottom of a deep, dark pit and couldn't climb out. Deep inside me, I wanted my own house. I deserved to be able to look out our windows. I didn't want postpartum depression. I also believed I was a terrible mom.

He is your deliverance and will saturate your thirsty soul.

Not even fifteen minutes later, my phone rang, and it happened to be one of my best friends and my spiritual mentor in college, Kristie. I immediately grabbed her call. As she spoke, her words flowed like a soothing balm to my soul. She listened to everything and responded with gentleness, understanding, and life-giving words. God used her to lift me up and set my feet on the road to healing.

Have you ever been in circumstances so difficult that you aren't sure God will make a way out? You're screaming for something different, better and, well … redeeming.

The people of Israel sure understood the need for divine deliverance. In Isaiah, God promises his people that something is going to be done in the world that has never been done before—the redemption of mankind through the Messiah. This "new thing"—Israel's deliverance—would be greater than the famous rescuing of the nation of Israel from the hands of Pharaoh in Egypt.

In the days of Moses, the power of God delivered one nation and *one* people from the hand of a tyrant through the salvation of rushing waters at the Red Sea. When the feet of Christ gripped the sands and rock leading him to Calvary, God's divine power and love brought salvation to *all* the nations through the blood of Christ.

In your own times of waiting in the wilderness, your hope is in your Savior who shed his tears when he gasped his final breaths, "My God, my God, why have you forsaken me?" (Matthew 27:46). The bitter tears of victorious Jesus are an endless supply of refreshing rivers for your weary soul. He is your deliverance and will saturate your thirsty soul.

Have you tasted this water that brings us new life? He'll provide your every need and make a way where there seems to be no way.

Prayer

Jesus, I confess that I don't always like my circumstances. I've complained, wanting to wear a different pair of shoes. I'd rather travel the easy road than one of struggle and suffering. But I know you have plans for me in the pain. Grow me in the times I want to give up and not trust you. Strengthen me as I wait upon your deliverance. Amen.

DAY 3

Coffee Cravings

"For where your treasure is,
there your heart will be also."
Matthew 6:21

A few years ago, what started as a quick fix to nights of sleep deprivation therapy happily provided by my newborn, and 1-, 3-, and 5-year-olds, suddenly became a regular comfort and routine investment. In the many days of being up at night awakened by crying, hungry babies or wet beds, I found myself drawn to warm, sweet cups of caffeine at the Starbucks drive-thru that was conveniently located next to my son's kindergarten. I could smell the coffee beans on the way to drop off. This was especially tempting since I didn't have to unbuckle my other kids out of their car seats.

Now you might be wondering, *what's the big deal? That's not bad—you were an exhausted mom* (yes!). But there's no greater truth teller than when you begin to track your expenses and find out just how much you've invested in toasted marshmallow lattes. My heart was truly where my money was, and I found that my habits didn't help my waistline, budget, or marital conversations!

Money is definitely an issue that makes us squirm in our seats, isn't it? It's highly personal and attached to our emotion, character, and behavior. Money touches everything in our life it seems—we can't do much without it. If we spend any time reading the Gospels, we will find that Jesus sure didn't shy away from talking about finances. He gave us many principles and guidelines in Scripture. Money is mentioned over 800 times—more than anything else except for the kingdom of God.

Wherever we begin putting our money, our heart flows to it and thinks of it. We can still enjoy life, a pumpkin spiced latte, a pedicure, an Amazon deal, or cute kids clothes, but we need to be discerning in what we're giving our hearts to. We need to be vigilant about what consumes our thoughts and minds, puts us into bondage and consumer debt, and causes mistrust in our relationships. Jesus is telling us where we put our money is a very good indicator of what direction our hearts will go. The heart always follows the money. What is written in our checkbook and on our bank account is a marker of what we're giving ourselves to and what we love most.

> The less you give yourself to in this world, the more you are free to serve your King.

Jesus cares deeply about the state of your heart being at rest—free from the love of money and coveting what others have. The less you give yourself to in this world, the more you are free to serve your King. Anything that is choking the life out of you, he desires to free you from so you can experience fullness of joy, peace, and the ability to give generously to others.

Prayer

Father, you're my ultimate provider and the one whom I'm truly dependent on. When the lusts and cravings for more are consuming, give me the strength to resist and submit to your Spirit. Help me guard my heart and use the resources you've given me wisely. Amen.

DAY 4

Soul Solace

"Come to me, all who labor and are heavy laden, and I will give you rest. Take my yoke upon you and learn from me, for I am gentle and lowly in heart, and you will find rest for your souls. For my yoke is easy and my burden is light."
Matthew 11:28–30

Sometimes there are heated conversations my husband and I have that are recurring through the years:

Jeremiah: "Honey, you need to take a load off your feet. Come sit with me and rest for a minute."

Samantha: "Rest? What does that even mean? I can't rest when a child's always begging for my attention. How can I not be bothered? Rest isn't a part of motherhood. There's just too much to get done!"

Jeremiah: "Babe, please come sit down with me."

And then out of my mouth come more excuses as to why I can't sit down: laundry, dishes, cleaning, homework, dinner prep, work, exercise, goals, relationships, and the empty refrigerator.

It dawned on me recently, though, that he might be right. I rarely sit down, just to sit, not look at Facebook, the news, or the stained carpet that needs scrubbing. I'm controlled by my to-do list, and it has its grip on me as if it were alive.

So in the last few weeks, I started practicing the art of stopping and either lying down to rest or just sitting in our recliner. To my surprise, it gave me even more energy for the tasks ahead, got rid of my looming headache, and brought sweet cuddle time with my kids. I found real freedom in the moments of rest from the burden of my work.

Jesus knew what he was doing when he preached about rest, practiced it, and commanded us to have one day a week set aside where we do nothing—completely devoted to chilling out. He knows how quickly we get sucked into life's demands. We need solace not only physically but we need it spiritually.

"Come to me, all who labor and are heavy laden, and I will give you rest." The yoke of the Pharisees was opposite of Jesus' yoke. The Pharisees were offering people a list of regulations, legalistic law keeping, and self-righteousness as if those manmade laws would make them closer to God. They were focused on the outward works, instead of the depths of the human heart. Jesus was offering a yoke that was easy and light—not a burden of works-based righteousness that was impossible to meet and carry—because no amount of deeds we do can make us holier to God.

"… and you will find rest for your souls." The burden of keeping every jot and tittle of the law would be no more in Jesus. Jesus promises that we can be set free from legalism and the long list of rules and find ease in him. In him, we're rescued from wrong thinking such as, *If I only did this or that, God would love me more. If I just keep all his commandments, then I will be on the right track.* Or, *how can God still accept me in my failures and brokenness as a mom?* Thank goodness, we don't have to earn God's love.

> You can be released from the weight of finding your identity in the work you do or don't do.

When the burdens and aches you experience are crashing over you like the billowing waves in the ocean, you can swim safely to shore and find your solace in Jesus alone. You can be released from the weight of finding your identity in the work you do or don't do. When you fall short even on your very best day, his sacrifice is sufficient.

Jesus' yoke saves you from the temptation to find acceptance in how you perform for him or for another person's standard of righteousness. Praise God we're saved not by our own good works but by grace through faith alone. And that's all we need to rest in.

Prayer

Father God, sometimes I think I can earn my salvation. I carry burdens of legalism that are impossible to carry. Give me wisdom and understanding in your freedom of grace. Thank you that you love me and accept me because of how you see me through your Son Jesus. Amen.

DAY 5

Friendship and Confession

"Therefore, confess your sins to one
another and pray for one another, that you
may be healed. The prayer of a righteous
person has great power as it is working."
James 5:16

About six months after my family and I settled into our home in a new state, I told my husband that I was lonely. I loved everything about where God had put us. The serenity, the beauty, the community, our church, and the simple way of life had my heart, but I still felt like something was missing. Authentic relationships and friendships have been important to me since I was a child.

"Well, I think you're going to have to be intentional in reaching out," my husband responded, being the logically minded man that he is.

I pouted a bit about it. "Well, I kind of want them to invite me …" I replied.

Then I remembered, *to make a friend you have to first be a friend.*

Deep down, I was waiting for an invitation. I already had several invitations from others, but I was caught in a "poor me" state of mind. I was also comparing myself to my new friends who were rooted in our town and seemed to have it all together. But nothing could be further from the truth.

Jesus calls us to not merely stuff our sins but to confess them to one another and to pray for each other.

As I became more purposeful in reaching out to my friends and sharing my own challenges, they began to open up to me and revealed their struggles with anxiety, depression, and addiction. I was amazed when not long after they expressed to me that I'd been an encouragement to them as they were to me.

Jesus calls us to not merely stuff our sins but to confess them to one another and to pray for each other. There was a point in my life as a teen that I thought just confessing to God through prayer was enough. Who needed (or wanted) to know my darkest secrets anyway? But I've learned that confession is an invitation for healing in your relationship to Jesus and others.

22

God already knows that we've sinned, but we're agreeing with him and seeking to turn from those sins and follow him. We acknowledge our wrong and seek to make it right. And it's through seeking forgiveness and God granting it to us that our prayers are heard. And those prayers have great power as the Spirit works within us.

To be fully known and fully loved is one of the greatest gifts you can have on this earth. It's a little taste of heaven. And I believe that's what God is after in biblical community and friendship with others. Healing comes when you're striving toward holiness and obedience to Jesus in community *together.*

Confession to friends who authentically love you and truthfulness in your prayers are essential to growth and healing, and once you've experienced such acceptance and grace, it's difficult to live any other way.

Prayer

Heavenly Father, my natural inclination is to isolate in my struggles, but I know real freedom and healing are found in confessing my sins to others. Help me to be deliberate in seeking out authentic community and to know others from the inside out. Amen.

DAY 6

Beautiful Feet

"And how are they to preach unless they
are sent? As it is written, 'How beautiful are
the feet of those who
preach the good news!'"
Romans 10:15

Recently, a friend of mine was raving about an all-natural tinted moisturizer she loved and was selling, so I decided to purchase it and try it for myself—also desiring to support her side income. After using it for several months now, I get her excitement. I love that it is light, hides blemishes, and enhances skin tone. It gets the job done if you know what I mean.

You've probably noticed that all kinds of products are being sold these days on social media. The best marketers often have a deep knowledge of their product, understand its value because of personal experience, and naturally get excited to share it with others.

But I can't help but wonder: What if we were this ecstatic about our Jesus, the Savior of our hearts, our Redeemer and first love? What if we were proclaiming his good news to everyone we knew? Perhaps we aren't talking about him because we don't have a better knowledge of him, lack a personal experience, or don't understand our need for him, and therefore we don't sense an urgency to tell others.

When we understand the good news ourselves and experience its benefits, we will most naturally tell others about it.

When we market a product, it's valuable to the one who needs it. Someone who has acne will be refreshed by a product that clears up pores. Someone who needs home remedies for sicknesses, ailments, and allergies might find relief in the health benefits of essential oils. In Jesus, we aren't selling a product; we have something far better. Deep within, we all have a need for love, acceptance, and security. The good news is that we have that in Jesus Christ.

"How beautiful are the feet of those who preach good news." When we understand the good news ourselves and experience its benefits, we will most naturally tell others about it. We can ask God to put our calloused, worn-out feet on the path of another mom who's hurting and broken so we can show her the hope that we've found in Jesus. As we're going, we can pray for divine appointments at the park, grocery store, our work places, coffee shops, sporting events, and more.

Sometimes the best conversation starters are a simple, "How are you doing today?" and letting others know we're genuinely interested. We can invite moms into our homes for playdates, go on an outing with our kids, make a meal, or invite someone to a church function. The opportunities to share Christ's love are endless.

Jesus calls us to be "sent out" to do his work. The woman at the well didn't realize the poor state of her spiritual condition, but after her encounter with Jesus, she understood. Her eyes were opened to the truth of the gospel. She told everyone in her town about the man who already knew everything about her and loved her still. She simply couldn't hold it in and spread his name far and wide.

So, where must you go? Who must you meet? What story will you share?

Prayer

Jesus, I don't always share your good news. I'm fearful, worried, and concerned with what people will think of me. Make me brave to share my faith and story with those who need to hear it. Even though my feet are worn and weary, you're the one that makes them beautiful as I follow you. Amen.

HOW *Beautiful*
ARE THE FEET OF
THOSE WHO PREACH
good
News
ROMANS 10:15

DAY 7

Make War

"Submit yourselves therefore to God. Resist
the devil, and he will flee from you."
James 4:7

M y friend Justis recently wrote on her Facebook wall:
"Satan, I ain't got time for that!" She just had her
second child, she and her husband are becoming foster parents,
and they're actively serving the Lord. Justis' ability to make
war allowed her to move on in spite of the adversity and lean
on the greater one within her.

We have an enemy who would love to tear apart our marriages,
discourage our families, and cause disunity, division, and all
kinds of setbacks. We don't have time for that! We have
husbands to support and children to care for. But we must

know that we have an enemy who would love to take the hearts of our very own children.

He's working in this world like never before and seeking whom he might devour. He knows his time is limited, and just as he deceived the hearts of Adam and Eve in the garden, he twists the truth today, deceptively claiming: *God's not good. He doesn't love you. He's keeping something from you.*

Give him all your concerns, tears, struggles, weaknesses, and not-together-ness.

We know this is far from the truth, but sometimes it's easy to believe. Sometimes he's so crafty that his deception is disguised as something "good" that isn't ultimately what's best for us. But we know that in Christ, we've been given everything we need for life and godliness. We have the ability to stand up against the enemy's tricks and schemes and temptations that come out of left field. Sometimes we have to make war—to be proactive in the fight, not sitting on the sidelines waiting for the attack to blindside us.

We're told to submit to God and put on the full armor of God. Just as you'd never step foot outside half-dressed (even though, like me, you might question if you actually put your clothes on for the day), you'd never go without all your armor on when you know darts will be thrown at you. We're called to be fully ready for battle against the Enemy. God's Word, the sword of the Spirit, is how we defeat him best.

Submit yourself to God's authority and control. Give him all your concerns, tears, struggles, weaknesses, and not-together-ness. Let him have all of you. Resist Satan and he'll leave you alone. This is what it means to make war. This is what we're called to do.

And if you must have a motto like my wise friend Justis, by all means write it on a sticky note and slap it on your mirror:

Satan, I ain't got time for that!

God is good. He loves you. He's come to give you abundant life.

Prayer

Heavenly Father, spiritual warfare is often beyond me. It's hard to understand why it happens and how to combat it. Please give me discernment to know when something is not of you. Give me the power to resist Satan and stand firm in my faith. Amen.

DAY 8

Bloom

"Rejoice always, pray without ceasing, give
thanks in all circumstances; for this is the
will of God in Christ Jesus for you."
1 Thessalonians 5:16-18

It's been a year and a half now since God called our family away from the giant city of Dallas with all its abundant amenities and planted us in a tiny rural town called Holyoke, Colorado—two and a half hours east of Denver, 125 miles away from the nearest Starbucks and Target, and where you see more brown cows than people. God called my husband to serve our wonderful church as senior pastor. I've loved the transition, simple way of life, and wide-open spaces. My kids are thriving here, and we love the people and community. It has become home to us.

Occasionally when I'm tempted to doubt where God has placed us, I remember a conversation Jeremiah and I had with my parents' friends Dick and Sue who've been married for 54 years.

"Wherever she was, she made friends and made the most of where we were," Dick said. "My wife bloomed where she was planted."

Dick shared how wherever they'd moved and settled, Sue made a critical choice. Her contentment, not complaints, greatly impacted him as a man moving up the ladder in his career. He credited his success to her choice to be at peace in her circumstances.

Can you imagine your life right now being completely at peace with God in where he's placed you? Can you picture getting ready each morning, scrambling to get your kids dressed for the day, rushing out the door, and knowing for certain that God has a mission for you right where you are as a busy mom? I know I want to be there.

Joy is the idea that we bloom where we're planted.

We're called to rejoice always, pray continually, and give thanks in all circumstances—always! When our husbands aren't cooperating like we want, when our children disobey, and when we can barely scrape our feet out of bed in the morning—we rejoice. Really?

Many of Paul's epistles were written from a cold, dark, and damp prison cell. If anyone knows how to be thankful in every situation, it is Paul. Scripture tells us that he "learned" the secret to contentment. It was a process and didn't come instantly. He had to be taught too.

When your bank account is sparse, give thanks. When you're in a conflict with another person, pray without ceasing. When you're undergoing an illness or unexpected trial, yes, you can still have the joy of the Lord deep within you. Like Paul, you too, can live abundantly through dire circumstances and still have the joy of the Lord as you're abiding in him.

If there's anything that should characterize our lives as Christ-followers, it isn't how many times we go to church or read our Bibles, but it's joy. Joy is the idea that we bloom where we're planted.

How are the fruits of the Spirit working themselves out in your life? Joy in you, as a believer isn't so much about you always being a joyful, happy person on the outside. It's about trusting his strength working in you—relying on the Holy Spirit to produce fruit in your life. In spite of your circumstances, you learn peace and contentment by choosing joy.

Prayer

Jesus, joy is difficult when the waves and trials of life, loving my husband, and raising my children are difficult to balance. Help me to learn contentment and to have a joyful attitude among the chaos in my home.

Show me ways I can begin focusing on what you've already given me. Amen.

DAY 9

The Best Blueprint

"And so train the young women to love their
husbands and children, to be self-
controlled, pure, working at home, kind, and
submissive to their own husbands, that the
word of God may not be reviled."
Titus 2:4-5

How are you doing today?" the handsome dad with his two kids asked me out of the blue while I pushed the big blue shopping cart holding my three kids.

I felt shy, but it also felt good to be approached as a run-down and exhausted mom. Maybe he thought I was pretty.

The Holy Spirit then nudged me not to entertain the attention I was receiving, so I determined to keep it short and not dwell on the situation. I thought of my hardworking husband, the father of my four children, who I loved with all my heart and soul and who loved me with everything.

"I'm fine, thank you. Have a good day," I replied.

I smiled and walked away, darting for the cleaning supplies aisle. I gathered up my frazzled emotions and prayed for God's help to honor my husband and flee temptation. I was thankful for the escape as the temptation had blindsided me.

Paul has a lot to say to us as wives in just a few short verses. He calls us to not only love our husbands and children, but "to be self-controlled, pure, working at home, kind, and submissive" to our husbands. That's a pretty loaded verse with some amazing truth.

When we're *self-controlled* we're careful to keep ourselves disciplined in our thought life, actions, and words. We're able to lead ourselves well and to know when we need to flee a hazardous situation.

To be pure ... free from the pollution of the world, whether it's the distortion of God's design for sexuality, adultery, pornography, or allowing the marriage bed to be defiled. We're called as wives and mothers to be free from the lusts of our flesh, impurity, idolatry, and immorality. Anything that attempts to break the physical, emotional, and spiritual bond between us and our husbands should be annihilated.

We're called to love our husbands in such a way that we have a holy lust for them alone. We're called to do our part, even when we're exhausted from the long days, to sexually pursue our husbands and be his fantasy. After all, that's what we were when we said, "I do." That's what we can be to him now.

We're called to love our husbands in such a way that we have a holy lust for them

Working at home, kind, and submissive. Whether our role is working inside or outside the home, a little bit of both, or being a stay-at-home mom, we're all given the tremendous responsibility and privilege to manage the affairs of our household. This also involves looking after the hearts of our children and doing our best in making sure our homes are places of safety, acceptance, and security—with kindness and love as the Spirit works in us.

Being *submissive to our own husbands* involves honoring their leadership and respecting them as they answer to God. Submission isn't a dirty word as much as our culture has painted it to be, but it's God's beautiful design for a healthy, thriving marriage. Husbands and wives are equal in value, but distinct in their roles and responsibilities. This idea actually comes from God himself as the Father, the Son, and the Spirit each have distinct roles but are equal in being. Imagine if God the Son said to the Father, "No thanks. I'm not going to the cross for her!" But he did.

Of course, as wives and moms born with a sinful nature, we fall short. We don't always follow God's ways. We rebel against God's perfect design for marriage. The good news is that the word "train," means it's a process of discipline, time, and sanctification. It doesn't happen overnight, and it's not a quick fix. Older women, whether spiritually or by their age, are called by God to teach the younger women.

If you feel far from God's instructions for you as a mother and wife, you're not alone. We're all works in progress. But God doesn't want you to stay where you are. His Word gives you exactly what you need to succeed. This blueprint is provided for you in order to best serve your husband and children and is for your utmost good. It's truly a beautiful thing when you follow God's flawless plan.

Prayer

Jesus, sometimes I'm a hot mess in my marriage and raising my kids. I'm strong-willed and resistant to my husband's leadership. I fail a lot. But I know you have a perfect plan for how I relate to those I love best. Give me the strength I need to live in purity and respect toward the man I love. Thank you for the gift of marriage. Amen.

DAY 10

Shake It Off

"Have I not commanded you? Be strong
and courageous. Do not be frightened, and
do not be dismayed, for the Lord your God
is with you wherever you go."
Joshua 1:9

It was a slightly cold and rainy morning as I carried my newborn baby into T.J. Maxx to buy some fall decorations. His soft blue blanket was covering him in his carrier for the ten seconds we walked from our SUV to the store. And then, an elderly lady brushed by me and said these words:

"You need to get something on your baby's hands!"

I looked down at his precious, tiny fingers and sure enough they were bare. I held my tongue for a few seconds.

"Well, it's not too cold out. He's okay," I said trembling with my words.

I assured her that I was watching out for his good. I was his mommy, and that was the end of our unexpected conversation.

As I walked through the automatic doors, I felt like a horrible mom who didn't do the right thing—not to mention I was brand-new at all this and did care about what people thought. I felt timid and fearful in my new role, and her criticism stung, spoiling my mood as I shopped.

At the heart of the Christian life is learning to trust that God is with us wherever we go. God was with Joshua to lead the Israelites into the land of Canaan and to observe all that he had commanded in the Law of Moses. God made his promises to Joshua. No matter how hard it would get, he would be with him and lead and guide him as the newly appointed leader. He would be faithful to complete his work through him even in the midst of opposition and anguish.

At the heart of the Christian life is learning to trust that God is with us wherever we go.

Whatever we face as new or seasoned moms, God is with us. We don't have to fear people, judgments, comments, or criticisms as we raise our children. It's far too easy to look around and see what others are doing and saying and to act accordingly, but the opinion we should be seeking the most is God's. He is our standard. Our identity. And the one we look to for guidance when we're afraid and unsure.

When you live in such a way and a snarky or cutting comment is dished at you, you can brush it off, speak the truth in love, and be confident that God's with you and it will be okay. You can "shake it off" knowing that those words don't define or deter you from moving forward in doing the best you know how as the mother of your children.

God has appointed you in this sacred role. He's with you. Keep your eyes and heart focused on him.

Prayer

Jesus, I confess that I care too much about what people think. I measure myself against others. Teach me what it means to follow your leading and to have the courage to put my identity in you and not in what the world says I should be doing. Thank you for always being with me, even when I don't always feel it. Amen.

DO NOT TREMBLE
OR BE DISMAYED
FOR THE
Lord
your
God
IS WITH YOU.
JOSHUA 1:9

DAY 11

Controlled Chaos

"Whoever is slow to anger is better than the mighty, and he who rules his spirit than he who takes a city."
Proverbs 16:32

It was one of those days. My 3-year-old daughter was in a destructive mood, throwing things and screaming. She'd already banged her head into our hardwood floors that morning from not getting her way. I was sitting on the couch, and before I knew it, she launched a toy train straight at me and struck me right in the forehead. Tears welled up in my eyes from the pain. I looked into her bright blue eyes and screamed her name. My blood was boiling inside. I ran to discipline her, anger and rage filling my heart and actions.

This was just one of the *many* incidents of the past months. Constant disobedience, name-calling, feisty fits over how I squeezed the mustard on her hot dog or what hat I put on her head or how her socks were too thick and her refusing to wear them so we could never get out the door.

I could never satisfy her. No matter how hard I tried, she refused my help. I immediately got up to discipline her, and I felt like it was just never going to end with her behavior. You could call me a closet crier; I was by all means one of them. And I won't lie; a good cry is sometimes the best medicine.

> A mom who controls her own spirit, desires, passions, and lusts of the flesh is greater than a mighty warrior.

Proverbs says that a slow-to-anger, or patient, person is better than a warrior. How about a patient *mom* is better than a warrior? In other words, we can be the strongest man or woman, with the ability to conquer and dominate entire cities and kingdoms, but if we don't have control over ourselves and the beast raging within, it means nothing. A mom who controls her own spirit, desires, passions, and lusts of the flesh is greater than a mighty warrior.

We have the ability to either let our flesh take over in the heat of the moment or submit to the Spirit and be patient with our children. Before we discipline and correct our children, we can take a time-out and ask for God's help. We can reach out to a friend and ask for her prayers. We can go hide in a spot where our kids can't find us so we can cool off. Much of it is believing God can and will help you have control when the first thing you want to do is lash out at the offense done to you or to someone else.

We can also consider taking a deeper look at the root issue of our anger and rage. Are we feeling personally attacked, unloved, and insecure or sensing a loss of control, or is our pride and self-worth at stake? Many times, the outward signs of our rage reveal an unseen struggle deep down. Perhaps recognizing that patience never comes easy and truly is a miracle when it does happen gives us hope that God can help us.

Today, my Rebekah is a sweet six-year-old Kindergartner. She does her homework without me asking, doesn't stop moving, and is highly artistic. She's grown in communicating her needs with me and the fits and meltdowns are fewer. When channeled in the right direction, I've seen her strong will be such a gift to our family and others. She also teaches me more about myself everyday.

We'll face various battles in each new developmental stage with our children. Thankfully, the seasons are short. There's much wisdom in practicing the art of patience as our children navigate their own roller coasters. God isn't finished with your children yet. Most of all, he isn't finished with you!

Prayer

Dear God, anger is my natural response when I've been attacked or offended and situations are spinning out of control. Give me the patience that only comes from you to rule my spirit and submit to you when disciplining and teaching my children your ways. Thank you for the hope that this isn't the end of my story. Amen.

DAY 12

Baby Body

"I appeal to you therefore, brothers, by the mercies of God, to present your bodies as a living sacrifice, holy and acceptable to God, which is your spiritual worship."
Romans 12:1

S ometimes when I look in the mirror or see photos of my post-baby body times four, I cringe a little. I knew my body had changed dramatically through each unique pregnancy, but the full impact hits me when I see the proof. A squishy belly that my kids love to blow their sticky lips on, a larger pant size, purplish-blue varicose veins, stretch marks, and other unpleasant sights have surfaced that didn't exist before. I'm often amazed that my husband still finds me attractive after all my body has gone through.

I've often thought about what God would want us to know about our bodies. After all, he knows we've birthed a live human being into this world—many of us *multiple* human beings. We've fed our babies, clothed them, and watched over their very livelihood. We've sacrificed nearly 24 hours a day for them. Is the physical sacrifice we have made and are making worth it?

The new marks we wear are battle wounds that signify something so much greater than the eye can see. Of course there's nothing wrong with watching carefully what we eat, exercising, and eventually burning off the weight, but honoring God in that process is most important. We could be consumed with our health where it's an idol, or we might not be concerned at all, which isn't good either.

The truth is that our baby bodies, no matter what shape and size, are pleasing to the Lord. They reveal the physical, emotional, and spiritual sacrifices we make for our children every day. They signify the new life we've prepared for, prayed over, and laboriously delivered into this world. They remind us of the reward we have in raising our children and offering them to the Lord each day.

> Giving up the right to yourself in order to invest selflessly into the life of your precious child is a beautiful thing.

We're called to offer our bodies as living sacrifices unto the Lord, holy and acceptable. This is our act of worship to him. Worship to him isn't reserved just for Sunday mornings but is a lifestyle throughout the week. The physical sacrifices of putting our children's needs before our own, nursing our baby around the clock, easing the pain of a sick one, changing multiple diapers, losing sleep, cleaning up messes, managing meltdowns, watching over their safety, and more are all sweet sacrifices God sees and delights in.

Giving up the right to yourself in order to invest selflessly into the life of your precious child is a beautiful thing. Giving your body wholly to God and honoring him as you raise your children is an act of love and service to him that should never be devalued and diminished. God sees your effort and delights in it.

Prayer

God, my body is yours to do with as you please. Help me to honor you today and remember the great sacrifice I'm making as I invest in the lives of my children. I give myself wholly to you to do as you will in my life. In Jesus' name, amen.

DAY 13

Open Door

"Show hospitality to one another
without grumbling."
1 Peter 4:9

A fresh-from-scratch poppy seed Bundt cake for our neighbors, a trusted place to drop off your kids for a few hours, a glass of sweet tea to cool you off, or just a place to sit and talk, that was the atmosphere my mom created in my home growing up in the Carolinas. One of the greatest gifts my mom gave my dad, sister, and me growing up and continues to radiate in is hospitality.

My high school friend Jen would often say, "Every time I come in your kitchen, I want to e-e-a-a-t!" The aroma smelled like an apple pie endlessly baking in the oven. Every Thanksgiving and Christmas, our table was set like the front cover of a Williams-Sonoma cookbook. Every glass cup, plate, and piece of silverware in its perfect place, gracefully decorated. Best of all, my mom made people feel accepted, special, and important—even the plumber. To this day, I love reminiscing about the environment she created for us.

Her youngest daughter, on the other hand (that would be me), has burnt broccoli and other dishes multiple times. I've misread ingredients. I once made a chocolate cake that made my friend Mallory nearly choke to death due to baking soda overload. I've dished out the weirdest concoctions on the dinner table. I'm not always the neatest in my home. I'm clean, but a bit cluttery. I blame it on being creative. Showing hospitality makes me shake in my boots, gives me anxiety, and causes my control-freak tendencies to protrude.

So when I read verses like 1 Peter 4:9, I'm both challenged and convicted. Scripture clearly teaches that as Christ-followers we're to practice being hospitable to one another. Key word: Practice. *Yeah right*, you may be thinking. *My house is a disaster, macaroni is glued to my floor, I haven't vacuumed in months, and don't you dare step a foot in my filthy bathroom!* I'm right there with you.

The clincher, though, is that we're taught to do this "without grumbling"... Murmuring is *the expression of secret and sullen discontent.* In other words, it is a form of covetousness—having desire for something God has not given you. Not trusting God for what he has given you. Hospitality isn't drudgery but is a gift from God, and we have incredible opportunities to change the world through this gift in a way that nobody else can. In this way, hospitality can be freely offered with joy and without complaining.

When our doors are open, others can sense a belonging and a welcoming that is difficult to find in this cold, dark, and lonely world. When our home is accessible to outsiders, whether that includes our mom friends, their children, our kids' friends, neighbors, or strangers, it communicates, "I welcome you. I love and accept you. I invite you in." This is the gospel lived out in one of the most practical, tangible ways.

> **When our doors are open, others can sense a belonging and a welcoming that is difficult to find in this cold, dark, and lonely world.**

An open door also invites others into the craziness of our own life. It doesn't always have to be complicated either. If dinner is too overwhelming, sharing a cup of tea or coffee will do. If the house is a mess, inviting them to sit next to the overflowing pile of laundry can suffice. I've done that many times. People will see you for what your home life is really like and recognize you're pretty normal after all.

I'm convinced that if we waited until our home was pristine and picked up, we'd never welcome anyone inside. Practicing hospitality is a gift to others and an opportunity for others to know the real you. Who's God calling you to invite in to the four corners of your beautiful mess? Chances are good that in turn, you'll be invited into their mess too.

Prayer

Jesus, my natural bent is toward selfishness. I'd rather isolate myself than invite others in to see my reality. Give me the desire to reach out and be a welcome mat for others so they'll see your love and goodness. Amen.

Show *Hospitality* to one another without grumbling.

1 Peter 4:9

DAY 14

Me, Too

"Two are better than one, because they
have a good reward for their toil. For if they
fall, one will lift up his fellow. But woe to him
who is alone when he falls and has not
another to lift him up!"
Ecclesiastes 4:9-10

One afternoon my friend Vanny was over at my house for a play date with her two girls. We'd known each other for a couple years and always seemed to naturally connect on a deeper level. I felt like I needed to be more vulnerable and share with her my recent struggles.

We stood in my kitchen slicing pieces of chocolate chip banana bread for our kids, and I decided it was time to share my burden. My heart raced, and I let it out:

"I've been cussing to myself and sometimes out loud from all the pressure that's on me as a mom and feeling so overwhelmed."

Vanny was now the first to know, along with my husband. She looked at me with eyes of understanding and compassion, not the judgment I feared.

"I get it. I do, too, at times."

I couldn't believe it. She struggled with this too?

When a burden is shared, that burden is divided and our load is significantly lighter.

I slowly felt the burdens of guilt, shame, and fear being lifted off my chest. And the truth was that I didn't have a cussing problem. I had a heart problem. Spewing careless words from my lips revealed a deeper struggle with control and anger over things not going my way. I felt I just couldn't meet all the needs of my children at once, and I became a person I didn't want to be.

Part of our sanctification, joy, and meaning in the Christian life comes from God using other people who we can count on for hope and encouragement. Ecclesiastes says that two are better than one because who will be able to help us if we fall and are alone? When a burden is shared, that burden is divided and our load is significantly lighter.

Our work is also better when it's completed together where we sharpen one another, edify, and hold each other accountable. The profit from our work is higher, and we're more successful when we have others to lean on and learn from.

Following Christ is better when we share our spiritual journey with others. He's created us to know others and be known by others. Because God knows our need for relationships and being connected to others, we can trust him that two really are better than one—it's one of his greatest blessings to us.

Prayer

Jesus, thank you for how you use others to sharpen us for our good and when we need a friend to pick us up. Help me be the kind of friend I desire to have and to live in community with others in a meaningful way. In your name, amen.

Part Two

Quieted by His Love

A TRANQUIL HEART
GIVES *Life*
TO THE FLESH, BUT ENVY
MAKES THE BONES ROT.

PROVERBS 14:30

DAY 15

H. A. L. T.

"Above all, keep loving one another
earnestly, since love covers a
multitude of sins."
1 Peter 4:8

One day recently, I woke up feeling like a wreck. I went on a morning run to get rid of the mess inside of me, but even after listening to worship songs and working up a sweat, I was tired, cranky, emotional, and irrational in my thought life. I couldn't escape it all day long no matter how hard I tried.

If you've ever heard of the H. A. L. T. acronym, which stands for hungry, angry, lonely, and tired, you know that danger's creeping at your door when you have one, two, three, or all of these going on. And you truly need to halt! My issue was the T. My husband and children took the brunt of my exhaustion. My words and actions weren't exactly a reflection of the magazine-cover mom.

I felt like giving up as a wife and mom. It felt good not to hold my tears in. *My sins are numerous*, I thought. *I just can't get it together. Everywhere I turn I create a disaster!*

Well, if you've found yourself in the eye of a storm you've created, it can be so discouraging when your sinful nature isn't tamed and you feel like there are some sins you'll never be able to overcome. In these moments, 1 Peter 4:8 helps us to overcome the Enemy's lies.

I drew upon this truth because the lies in my head were: *You're not good enough. You can't handle this. God is ripping you off. You will never overcome.*

And then in that moment God's Word began to flood my soul with life-giving truth: *You can handle everything in my strength. You are loved by me. I have come to set you free. I will help you overcome.*

> **Truth tells us that no matter how far we stray, love still covers a multitude of sins.**

Truth tells us that no matter how far we stray, love still covers a multitude of sins. Even on our very worst days, the perfect love of Jesus still covers the darkest corners of our homes—the ugly moments that bring shame and guilt. This kind of love also works powerfully within us when we've failed those we love dearly.

The 1,000 moments of love in a week that we've bestowed on them still trump the 100 sins that have made us feel like an absolute failure.

There's no sin that hasn't been covered by his blood, and because we're loved so much by our Savior, our response should be to give that love in return. This is the depth of love that we're called to receive from Jesus and give to others when we've failed to HALT.

Jesus understands your brokenness. His love never stops covering you—day in and day out. If you've found yourself swallowed by your own wake of disaster and exhaustion, know that you're loved, forgiven, bought at a high price, and set free from your sin. And by all means, *HALT* when you need to.

Prayer

Jesus, thank you that you provide a way of escape when we need it most. Thank you for your great love and for covering over my sins. Help me to rise above my failures and trust you more for the strength I need. Amen.

DAY 16

Good Grace

"May grace and peace be multiplied to you
in the knowledge of God
and of Jesus our Lord."
2 Peter 1:2

It was a crisp morning outside and my kids and I had just settled in for our daily routine at the park. The gentle breeze brushed against my cheek as I picked up my 17-month-old daughter and inched her little legs into the holes of the swing. My three-year-old son was happily playing on the slides.

The mom next to me pushed her little boy in his swing. She looked a few years older than I with long blonde hair and a pleasant smile.

"I can't believe you're going to have another one!" She initiated the conversation.

Oh, here we go again, I thought.

I'd heard this before from other people in public who I didn't know in our big city. I was agitated, but I tried my best to be nice.

"Yep, it will be a lot as they are all close in age," I replied.

I talked a little bit about the challenges I knew I'd face as a mom of three young children. And that, yes, it was crazy. Then I switched the subject and asked her questions. She was happy to tell me about her kids and how she could never have them back-to-back. And I understood her completely.

But what that mom didn't know about me was that I had huge fears and worries when it came to welcoming our third baby that June. I had a rough transition from one to two kids, and since this baby was only 20 months apart from my youngest, it brought a lot of "what ifs" in my head. I was scared of how I would juggle the demands.

> Grace—God's unmerited favor, goodwill, and loving-kindness toward us as imperfect sinners.

How would I handle three meltdowns? Three whines for Mommy? Three hands pulling on my legs? Three bedtime routines? And going out in public with three all at once? I didn't know what I was getting myself into. And then as if to write itself across the sky, I felt the Lord tenderly speaking the word:

G R A C E !

God's unmerited favor, goodwill, and loving-kindness toward us as imperfect sinners. Not only is grace ours to behold in our relationship with Christ, but peace is, too, and in abundance. His grace is enough in my relationship to Jesus, and it would be enough for me as a mom of young children.

No matter what kind of day you've had, it's his grace that keeps you going even when you don't feel it or even realize it's there for the taking. His grace helps you live in the Spirit and love your children well, holds you when you can't do anything in your own strength, and is what you cling to in your desire to be a better wife, mom, and friend.

God's grace looks different for each of us and the various loads we carry each day, but we've all been given "grace upon grace" in our lives (John 1:16). It is continuous, never ceasing, and always available for us to draw upon. It never runs out even when we've run ourselves ragged! Perhaps, we just need to cut ourselves some slack, worry less about tomorrow's stress, and lean into his good grace just for this very hour.

$Prayer$

Jesus, I need your abundant grace every day. Help me to rest in the promise of your love for me when I feel defeated and my burdens are crushing me. Thank you that your grace has held me and will continue to do so in the future. In your name, amen.

Grace & Peace BE YOURS *in abundance* THROUGH THE KNOWLEDGE OF *God* & OF *Jesus* OUR LORD.

2 PETER 1:2

DAY 17

Interrupted Plans

"The heart of man plans his ways, but the
Lord establishes his steps."
Proverbs 16:9

T he heart of man plans his ways, but the Lord establishes
his steps." We have all kinds of thoughts and plans inside
our minds, don't we? I've told God many times what I think he
should do. But thank goodness, he is the one that fulfills what
is to be in my life.

Three years ago, our fourth baby Will was born on a beautiful
August Monday morning in Dallas. Nine months prior to that, I
was on birth control and exclusively breastfeeding. I'll never
forget the moment when I found out that I was expecting. My
calm and laid-back third baby, Hannah, was only four months
old.

And I cried; oh, did I cry. I questioned. I even threw my pregnancy test across the room. How in the world could I be ready for a fourth child—right after giving birth to Hannah? I barely had time to recover. I was numb and in disbelief, more so thinking about how I'd be able to carry the load I already couldn't seem to bear. Jeremiah and I desired to have four children but had wanted to wait a few years.

Would I take God at his word? Would I trust him for the strength I needed to survive life with four children, five and under? Ultimately, would I accept this surprise gift as God's sovereign will

But it is often in these diversions we remember we are not in control.

for my family and me? It was only a matter of days when God clearly showed me to be still and to relinquish control.

I accepted this precious gift from God's hands and kept giving the baby inside me to God. It was a great testing of my faith. After his birth and now as he's three years old, I'm so thankful God interrupted my plans, because William is the biggest blessing to our family.

When God modifies our plans, it is uncomfortable, and many times fear and worry consumes our hearts: an unplanned pregnancy, a job change, an unexpected illness, a detour in daily plans, a career change, or perhaps a waiting period that is just too long. But it's often in these diversions we remember we are not in control. We can't be dependent on our circumstances, on people, or even ourselves. We can't manipulate God's will. In these moments, we have to make a choice:

Surrender or become bitter.

We can murmur, complain, get angry, throw things, and stew on the disappointment. We can reject his leading. Or we can trust that even though we don't understand what we've been given, God is working for our good and deeply loves us.

One of the greatest things we can learn when plans don't go our way is humility. Pride says, "I've got this figured out. I'm in control. I'm pretty good at knowing the way. I'm the master of my destiny." Humility says, "I don't have life figured out. I need a Savior whom I can depend on. I need his guidance and direction every moment of my life. I need Jesus in all of life's circumstances."

As our heavenly Father, he knows what's best for us and, yes, even what we can handle.

Prayer

Jesus, I admit that I love having control of the wheel to my life. But I know your plans and ways are far greater than my own. Teach me to trust you when my ideas are redirected. Thank you that you're working for my good even when I can't see what's ahead. Amen.

DAY 18

Fruitful Waiting

"And I am sure of this, that he who began a
good work in you will bring it to completion
at the day of Jesus Christ."
Philippians 1:6

One morning last spring as I was in the craziness of making scrambled eggs and bacon for everyone, I glanced outside our kitchen window and noticed the first few buds on our tree beginning to burst with flowers.

"Look kids! The flowers are budding!" I said.

They dropped what they were doing and ran outside to see. My son John snapped some photos on my phone of the new life before his curious eyes.

During the winter months, the hardened buds and lifelessness from the trees are all we see, but we know that in spring the buds are set up to blossom again. And much of the deadness all around us in the winter months actually protects the buds so they will sprout again and in the right time.

Similarly, I've gone through seasons of intense dryness spiritually where my soul is cold and numb to the Holy Spirit's work in my life. Where I don't thirst for Jesus, the Living Water, as I should. Where I don't treasure Jesus like I should or cling to his all-sufficient grace because I'm selfish and full of pride, the difficulties of life have choked me, and various idols fill my heart. I've questioned, *Is God even working in the cold, winter months of my soul? Is he here?*

God doesn't start something he won't finish.

I'm still in a season of struggle, or should I say, "struggling well," where I desire to be closer to Jesus and further away from my sin. But I know he is here just as sure as spring brings new life.

"He who began a good work in you will bring it to completion..." God doesn't start something he won't finish. He promises to finish his work in you. You may not see the fruit in the waiting, but you know he's working. You may not behold what you want to "now." You may not see change or growth in anger, control, and people-pleasing struggles right away, but it'll come. This process of God chastening, chiseling, and molding our character, behavior, and attitudes is indeed a process of patience.

You may not think you are growing or becoming a different person right now, but God sees the last paintbrush stroke on the canvas. He views the whole treasured portrait of your person, not merely the snapshots taken here and there of your successes and downfalls.

Even when your soul feels cold and barren, God can still make something beautiful in due time. Just like those buds exploding with new life, color, and vibrancy, God is fully able to work in your life in a way you've never experienced before.

Prayer

Jesus, I want to trust you with my life. Grow me in the months of my soul that are sapped and desert-like. Please give me patience while I wait on you to move. In your precious name I pray, amen.

DAY 19

Take Heart

"I have said these things to you, that in me you may have peace. In the world you will have tribulation. But take heart; I have overcome the world."
John 16:33

Every Sunday, Mike protected the doors to the children's ministry at our church. You could never walk through the entrance without feeling secure as he stood there proudly in his police uniform, hands clasped at his waist, with a gigantic smile on his face. He was a magnet for our children who often would run up to him and hug his legs and give him high fives. Mike was a tender warrior, loved by everyone he met.

On July 9, 2016, Mike left behind his wife and two daughters when he was killed in the line of duty. On the day of the tragedy, I balled like a baby and told my seven-year-old what had happened because I knew he remembered Officer Mike.

John was processing all that happened and was confused as to why anyone would want to kill a police officer.

"Mom, dad's safe being a pastor, right?" he asked me with concern, wanting to make sure his daddy was going to be okay while on the job. My heart ached from his question.

"We're safe in God's will," I responded. "That's the safest place to be."

Provision has already been made for our redemption and reconciliation to him.

I shared how anything can happen anywhere living in a fallen world full of sin. We talked more about safety, evil, and how one day God will redeem this broken world. He loves everyone equally and hates murder. It's difficult to explain to a child the evil permeating our land and how it just doesn't make sense but that God still turns horrible situations into good.

Jesus said that in this world, we *will* have trouble. It's not if, but when. And when trials come, we must trust it isn't the end of the story. Jesus has already overcome the world, and he comforts us in the pains of this life. Before time, his plan was to redeem mankind back to himself through his shed blood on the cross. He fulfilled that plan when Jesus completed his journey to the cross and was buried and rose again. Provision has already been made for our redemption and reconciliation to him. That should give us great peace. That is why he exhorts us, "Take heart!"

God isn't finished yet. When your thoughts are exhausted with fear, anxieties, and worry for your family's safety, health, and well-being, take heart in Jesus because he wins in the end. He'll fulfill his purposes and create something beautiful from the dust.

This world isn't as it should be, and this truth should humble us and give us great hope that restoration and redemption are waiting for us.

Prayer

Heavenly Father, I need you in this broken world. You're my steadfast peace. When fears choke the life out of me, help me to constantly give them over to you. Protect my family and children as we seek to do your will. Amen.

DAY 20

Joyful Provision

"Look at the birds of the air: they neither
sow nor reap nor gather into barns, and yet
your heavenly Father feeds them. Are you
not of more value than they? And which of
you by being anxious can add a single hour
to his span of life?"
Matthew 6:26-27

I can't say that I worry about the big things in life as often as
I do the little things: how my kids will do in school, if I'll
have enough energy to make a somewhat decent dinner, how
long it will take to clean up the mess afterwards, if I've reached
10,000 steps on Fitbit, or if I'll get enough sleep tonight.
Sometimes I find myself wishing that I didn't carry the weight

of burdens the Lord says he'll take care of. I mean, can I do a better job than he? I know I can't, but why do I try so hard?

I see and hear the birds outside my kitchen window. They're busy building, flapping their wings, and happily singing a tune—not having a care in the world about what's going on or where they'll acquire their food. Sometimes I just sit and watch them to see if I could be a little bit more carefree as they are.

God feeds and cares for the birds of the air. He's watching over them. And I am more valuable? Jesus says that I am. Since we're more precious than the birds, how much more does Jesus care about us and the daily details of our lives? Jesus desires us to trust in God's provision and plan for our lives—not just for the future but right now. For the next ten minutes, the next hour, and the next ten hours. We can trust him because he's a good Father who provides for his own.

Trusting in his goodness is a daily act of your will.

He knows that worry tends to choke the life and joy out of us. It gets us nowhere fast, doesn't solve anything, and is a waste of sweet time. Jesus understands our natural tendency to do the opposite of what we should do. He knows that we often try to numb the pain of anxiety, worry, and stress with things like busyness, wearing a mask of perfection, phone addiction, over-spending, finding comfort in food, or neglecting to deal with the root causes of our dissatisfaction.

When you know and believe that your heavenly Father is watching out for your best, loves you infinitely, and cares for every facet in your life, anxiety and worry begin to steadily take the back seat. Step by step, you begin to trust where God's taking you and how he's changing you for his purposes. Trusting in his goodness is a daily act of your will.

Like the birds of the air, may you live in freedom and unity with Jesus as you strive to better trust in your heavenly Father who knows exactly what you need and even want.

Prayer

Jesus, I worry about everything and it robs me of peace and joy. Forgive me for relying so much on myself and not on your grace and provision. Teach me to cast my burdens and cares on you so that I may live a life of trust, contentment, and gratefulness in you.

DAY 21

Loud Love

"The LORD your God is in your midst,
a mighty one who will save;
he will rejoice over you with gladness;
he will quiet you by his love;
he will exult over you with loud singing."
Zephaniah 3:17

I'm forever grateful to have been raised in a loving Christian home. My mom came to know the Lord early in her marriage through her friend and co-worker faithfully sharing Christ with her during their lunch breaks. My mom brought my sister and me to church every Sunday and Wednesday—even when I resisted and threw fits. Growing up, the highlight of my summer was going to camp.

Each summer, I'd rededicate my life to Christ because I felt that former school year I wasn't loving God well or being a good Christian. I must've rededicated my life three or four times around the campfire. I was young and didn't understand grace and a relationship with Jesus, but I knew I was a sinner and I strived to please the Lord.

In the back of my mind, I'd felt like God's love was conditional: If I did this or that, then he'd love me. I thought when I failed I'd be struck down by a lightening bolt from heaven. Of course, that was far from the truth. As I grew in age and in my faith, I began to understand his love more. Now in my 30s, I'm still trying to grasp a proper perspective of how God views me through his Son Jesus.

God's love is like that of a father who'd do anything and everything to be with you. Like the father of the prodigal son, he watches and waits for you. He doesn't force you to choose his love either. But since you are his, he pleads with you to know how much you're *already* loved.

In Scripture, the prophet Zephaniah reveals that the good news of the gospel is available not only to Jews but to Gentiles also. We're all heirs of the promise through faith, and that is a mystery worth singing about.

Not only are you grafted in as a daughter of God, but also he delights in you as his child and magnificent creation.

Not only are you grafted in as a daughter of God, but also he delights in you as his child and magnificent creation. He rejoices over you with singing. Your Creator, who spoke the world into existence with his spoken word, also sings over you. This isn't just a soft lullaby like you'd sing your baby to sleep, but this is loud singing with excitement and rejoicing. It's a party!

I have days where I wish God wasn't seeing my behavior and attitude toward my husband and children. I think I'm a horrible mom and not worthy when I yell at my kids, imitate their disrespectful behavior, or tear them down with my words. Or when my attitude toward my husband is mean and selfish. How could God rejoice over me in my nastiness? He really loves me that much? Really? Yes, he does—and he's already proven his love by coming to earth, dying on a cross, and granting me the free, costly gift of salvation.

Not only is he mighty to save you from all your sins past, present, and future, but he's in your midst. He's with you right now. Whatever trial and hardship you're enduring, he's here and takes great delight in you just as he takes great joy in his name. Let him sing over you as you go about your day. Even among the noise and mayhem in your midst, let him quiet you with his unwavering, unconditional love.

Prayer

Jesus, your gospel has changed me, and because of your goodness, I've been made right with you through faith. Help me live my life in light of your rejoicing over me. Even though my righteousness is as filthy rags, you still take great pleasure in me and love me unconditionally, and for that I'm so grateful. I love you, amen.

HE WILL REJOICE OVER
YOU WITH
Gladness ;

HE WILL QUIET YOU
BY HIS
Love ;

HE WILL EXULT OVER YOU
WITH LOUD
Singing

ZEPHANIAH 3:17

DAY 22

Second Nature

"Delight yourself in the Lord, and he will
give you the desires of your heart."
Psalm 37:4

D o you ever wonder if God has forgotten about your
dreams and desires as a mom? I sure do. The grimy
dishes, overflowing laundry, sassy mouthing, defiant behavior,
and expended energy are enough to make anyone go over the
edge and forget about their own hopes and dreams. But let me
fill you in on a secret: Those desires that burn wildly in your
heart aren't there by coincidence.

When we begin to delight ourselves in the Lord, it's as if his
desires become ours. When we're so in tune with God's Spirit
and getting to know him, it's almost like second nature to do

the things that he desires. I've seen at times that what I crave comes directly from what God is giving me a hunger for.

To delight means to bend toward, be inclined to, and take pleasure in. When we delight in God, we're concerned about his purpose and resolve in our lives. We take great pleasure in knowing him and seeking his will. As we grow in our faith, our desires also begin to change. What once looked pleasing to our eyes may not anymore because of God's work in us.

> **To delight means to bend toward, be inclined to, and to take pleasure in.**

When you're seeking God, loving him and taking pleasure in him, your bent toward sin and things that can harm you is lessened. When you're living for his purpose and are resolved to do his will alone, Scripture promises that you will find it. In his timing, he will bring it to pass. This isn't a prosperity gospel—that if you do this or that, God will bless you with health, wealth, and abounding happiness. This is about you aligning your desires with God's desires for you.

God hasn't forgotten you. He instills the dreams, passions, hopes, and longings inside you for a reason. Scripture says that you can come to the throne of grace with confidence and boldness to ask him anything you want. You can confidently, in child-like faith, ask God:

"What's your will for my life? What do you desire to accomplish through me in this season? What have you created me to do specifically here on earth?"

In time, as you delight in pleasing him and doing his will, he'll answer your deepest longings.

Prayer

Dear God, you've given me desires for a reason and purpose. I want to do your will and to fulfill those dreams. Please show me what they are and live them out in me. I want my desires to be yours. Thank you for planting seeds in my heart that have yet to flourish but will yield fruit in due time. Amen.

DAY 23

Numbered Days

"So teach us to number our days that we
may get a heart of wisdom."
Psalm 90:12

Last year, my seven-year-old son John woke up one school morning in extreme pain and unable to walk. He limped and screamed every time he moved his right leg. I took him to the emergency room, and after the doctors ran tests and got a sonogram of his hip, they discovered he had fluid on his hipbone—something I'd never heard of. They told us we needed to drive an hour to another hospital to see if he would need surgery. My heart grew frantic, and all the "what ifs" settled in my mind.

After the long drive and checking him in, the doctor diagnosed John with toxic synovitus—a temporary condition that causes hip pain and happens typically in children ages three to eight years old (most common in boys). They gave him light anesthesia before the procedure, we waited, and then they drained the fluid with a needle. I was a nervous wreck with surgery always being in the back of my mind.

John made it fine through the procedure and after more hours of waiting, he was himself again and not in pain. We were relieved to hear that he wouldn't need surgery and we'd be discharged soon.

I was relieved. My firstborn was going to be okay. I was so thankful but still experienced highs and lows the week after from the traumatic experience. My first baby had always been healthy, and the thought of him being sick plagued me.

We're called to use our days wisely and invest with caution.

The incident reminded me that we aren't guaranteed anything when it comes to tomorrow. As we read in Psalms, God numbers all our days. He's the author and finisher of each one. He's entrusted us with our children, but we must continually give them back to God as an offering and act of worship. We acknowledge that everything we've been given is from the hand of God.

When life is smooth sailing, it's easy to think we're in control—that we have our days figured out—but wisdom tells us to hold each day delicately. We have an appointed time on earth that will come to an end.

We're called to use our days wisely and invest with caution. Some questions we might consider are:

In what ways can I purposely invest in the eternal souls of my children?

How can I use the power of God's Word to inform and guide their hearts for years to come?

How can I better help them love their friend and neighbor as they love themselves?

How can I equip them to stand up in a culture that's increasingly hostile to God and his ways?

The time you have with your children is short, and in a blink, they'll be getting their driver's licenses and you'll be releasing them from the nest. Because the days are long and the years are short, ask God to help you see life the way he sees it and to value each day even when it's difficult.

Prayer

Father God, I confess that the ordinary routines of life keep me from being focused on the eternal. Give me wisdom to think about each day as a gift and to handle it sacredly. Thank you for all that you have given to me. Amen.

DAY 24

Believe

"Then he said to Thomas, 'Put your finger here, and see my hands; and put out your hand, and place it in my side. Do not disbelieve, but believe.' Thomas answered him, 'My Lord and my God!' Jesus said to him, 'Have you believed because you have seen me? Blessed are those who have not seen and yet have believed.'"
John 20:27-29

I don't remember exactly what my preschooler had done that afternoon, but he was deliberately disobedient. He was pushing my buttons at just the right time. He continued with his defiance, and it was in that moment that I grabbed him and dug my nails in his neck. I lashed out, yelling like a crazy woman.

There's a point when we discipline for correction, and there's a line that we cross when we break a child's spirit. I'd done the latter.

Anger filled my heart. I wanted to quit. Guilt and shame flooded my soul for the way I'd hurt him. After cooling off and just wanting to hide in a corner, I confessed my sin to the Lord and to my son.

"I'm sorry, John. Mommy is struggling, and the way I treated you was wrong. Will you forgive me?"

"Of course, Mom. I love you," were his words.

Oh the forgiveness that I didn't deserve. But with welcoming, child-like faith he accepted my apology. He loved me anyway, and our relationship was restored.

Perhaps you're like me. You see your brokenness, humanity, and sinful nature for what it is, and it isn't pretty. You'd rather isolate and not expose it. You carry burdens of shame and guilt that seem unmanageable. I get it.

Jesus does too.

Because of the costly price of our sin, Jesus covered the enormous debt we couldn't pay. Because of our sin and weakness, he willingly went to the cross to be crucified. He suffered, he bled, and he died a criminal's death.

His love ran red for you. His blood on the cross took care of your sin problem. And his wounds heal you.

His wounds save you from the outbursts of anger, the covetousness, the discontentment, the lusts of your flesh, the need to control, the yearning for approval, the desire to have more, the itch to be successful, the intense struggle with your children, the pride, and more.

The gospel is also for the mom who is weary and trembling in her calling to raise up her children in the way they should go. He understands your struggle and suffering too. The truth is that we can't manage our sin in motherhood, but Jesus can. We don't have it all together, and we need someone greater.

After Jesus' victory over death and sin and after he rose from the dead, doubting Thomas still wavered in believing that Jesus was who he said he was—the Messiah. The Savior of the world. More importantly, *his* personal Savior.

> The gospel is also for the mom who is weary and trembling in her calling to raise up her children in the way they should go.

After the resurrection when Jesus was with his disciples, he said to Thomas, "Put your finger here, and see my hands; and put out your hand, and place it in my side. Do not disbelieve but believe."

Thomas had touched his Savior's wounds and he responded: "My Lord and my God!"

The proof was before his eyes. Jesus was the Son of God. He had no excuse not to believe. And Jesus said to him, "Have you believed because you have seen me? Blessed are those who have not seen and yet have believed."

There's much we don't see in our calling, but do we still believe that Jesus is who he said he is? Do we trust that his wounds have set us free from sin and will continue to pardon us in the hard days to come?

The burdens of shame and guilt you carry have been covered by Jesus' blood on the cross. You can live in victory over your sin by *his* strength and in *his* power. And he's fully able to help make you the woman you desire to be.

He sees you. He knows you. He's for you.

Prayer

Jesus, many times I'm a doubting Thomas. Rescue me from my unbelief. Give me the strength to trust you at your word even when I can't see you. Thank you for your shed blood on the cross and for my salvation. Amen.

DAY 25

Strong Mom

"He will tend his flock like a shepherd; he
will gather the lambs in his arms; he will
carry them in his bosom, and gently lead
those that are with young."
Isaiah 40:11

I was nervous and wondered what the other moms would think. Would they accept us if they knew who we really are? These were some of the thoughts I had when my husband and I had the opportunity to speak for my mother's group on the topic of marriage.

During our talk, I shared some stories of how our kids have impacted our relationship and how I struggle at times with anger and control in raising our four young children. Sharing the raw details of life can be a scary risk that requires vulnerability.

Afterwards, one of my friends who I respected and who, in my eyes, was a "super mom," came up to me and revealed how much she related to what I shared.

"Really?" I asked her.

"Yes, it's as if you were talking straight to me," she said. "I struggle all the time with anger. I yell a lot. And I'm so angry in my home."

That experience made me realize there's no such thing as a super mom, no matter if you have 19 kids or one. But I still wonder at times if some of my friends have special "supernatural momma abilities" I just don't possess.

There is, however, such a thing as a strong God, who is mighty, perfect, and all-powerful; does not grow weary; and is fully capable of helping you in your time of need.

But no matter if all seems well on the outside, we're still human with limitations, imperfections, and shortcomings. We grow tired, impatient, and cranky, and we desperately desire time to ourselves to escape the chaos of disciplining defiant behavior, managing our household, and much more. Sometimes the emotional side of motherhood can be so overwhelming.

We're only human.

There is, however, such a thing as a strong God, who is mighty, perfect, and all-powerful; does not grow weary; and is fully capable of helping you in your time of need. He knows how you're shaped, what discourages you, where you struggle, and who you are. He is well equipped to wrestle the battles for you.

As Isaiah promises, God is carrying you close to his heart and is gently leading you as you teach, guide, and train your children. He understands that this is a vulnerable, weary, and exhausting time of life, and he's here for you to lean on. His strength working itself in you is how you're able to be a strong mom. It's not within your own strength.

Remember that in your greatest moments of shame, anger, outbursts, wrestling with control, and fights with your flesh, you have a strong God who will fight for you and loves you deeply.

Prayer

Jesus, thank you that you are strong and will fight for me in my struggles. Help me to remember the truth that I need you every hour. Thank you for leading me as a young mom and being my loving and perfect Father. In your name, amen.

DAY 26

Nurtured and Satisfied

"Like newborn infants, long for the pure
spiritual milk, that by it you may grow up
into salvation."
1 Peter 2:2

Immediately after all my babies were born, they were quick
to let me know what their taste buds longed for. They
craved milk for what seemed like every hour of the day and on
into the night. Without that sweet, nourishing milk, they'd cry
out in absolute desperation. When their need was met, they
were the most satisfied babies in the world.

Desire. Frequency. Intensity. Savoring God's milk causes us to
mature in our faith. The rich and satisfying nutrients of this
"spiritual milk" are infused into us when we latch on to God

and drink of his kindness toward us. When we embrace the love of God and drink what he freely gives us, when the latch is broken we will fuss like babies because we want more. We'll desire it more and more. There will be intense cravings that only God can satisfy.

God's love is expressed most intensely through Jesus, revealed to us by his Word in the Bible, experienced in community with his people, and painted throughout creation. It helps us to "grow up" in our trust that God is a good Father. It compels us to love him. Spiritual milk is heaven on earth, the implant of God's nature in our life.

Tasting and savoring this kindness makes me grow up. It helps me to trust and to love my Savior Jesus and my fellow neighbor in a way that shows I am truly his.

This "milk" is truly the ways of heaven, the truth of God's mercy, and the help that comes to us and teaches us a better way to live. It's how we fully savor and enjoy the kindness of God, learning to trust him more each day.

Tasting and savoring this kindness makes me grow up. It helps me to trust and to love my Savior Jesus and my fellow neighbor in a way that shows I am truly his. I must know of this kindness. I must be convinced of its truth from the inside out.

Yet, I'm in danger. My heart and soul risk being malnourished through pride and selfishness and the lusts and impurities of this world. Turning to anger and isolation is like ingesting all the Cheetos, pizza, and ice cream at a party. It seems so good to take in but leaves us feeling bloated and empty with a waistline that taunts us, reminding us of our poor decision to unlatch from God's ways and eat from what doesn't satisfy.

It's the kindness of God that gently calls us to place our lips, drink freely, and experience life and vitality, security, and love. It's through this food we'll grow up in our salvation and nowhere else.

Therefore, we must strip away every delight and pleasure in this world except for a craving and intensity for the words of God. Let our hearts desire what God offers to us. For only here will we have all we need. We will be completely satisfied because *he* is all we need in this life. Once we have tasted his goodness and love in our life, it's difficult to desire anything else.

Prayer

Jesus, I want to know you more and delight in your Word. When I'm craving everything but you, give me the desire to read your Word and meditate on it as it brings life to my bones. Thank you for the gift of your Word and how it teaches me how to live. Amen.

LONG FOR THE PURE

Spiritual

milk

THAT BY IT YOU MAY
GROW UP INTO

Salvation

1 PETER 2:2

DAY 27

Broken Prayers

"For you did not receive the spirit of slavery
to fall back into fear, but you have received
the Spirit of adoption as sons, by whom we
cry, "Abba, Father."
Romans 8:15

I t's interesting how the word *prayer* conjures up many
emotions and feelings for people. You might view your
prayer life as a delight, a duty, or both. Maybe it just depends
on what kind of day you're having, but either way, prayer is a
gift that we have so we can hear from and speak with our
Father. And he delights to hear from us no matter what the
circumstance.

The responsibilities of working, raising children, serving in
ministry, and making our marriage a priority often leaves my

husband and me with no choice but to fall on our knees before God. Our prayer lives have been forced to grow as our demands have increased over the years, and I admit that much of my strength has come from confessing my absolute brokenness.

When I was single, I had a more designated time for prayer, but now my prayers are more unscheduled, short, and spontaneous. And lately the prayer I offer most to God is, *Help!* I've also had times when the only words I could offer were tears. The most pivotal prayer of all was when I asked Jesus, *Save me.*

Sometimes I still feel this pressure to offer drawn-out, formal prayers to God, and if I don't do this, I'm not spiritual or doing what he wants. But it's interesting to note that in Romans, Paul says that in our spirit we cry out, "Abba, Father" in our adoption as his children. And that's a short prayer if I've ever seen one. Two words to be exact.

We're to be natural with God. And sometimes our prayers are more like moans and groans and longings, just like we'd cry out to our own earthly father.

Short, broken prayers to God are enough when that's all we have to offer.

You can just picture the sound and pitch of the word "D-a-d-d-y" when your child's in great danger or in need of help, and when you cry "A-b-b-a" to your heavenly Father, it's the same. Like a loving father to his child, our heavenly Father tenderly and compassionately responds to our cry.

Short, broken prayers to God are enough when that's all we have to offer. Lots of things keep us from being wide open and real with God, including our pride, stubbornness, fear, inability to trust him with everything, and failure to believe he loves us.

But when you come to God as your Abba, tell him what he already knows, and be real with him; you'll be amazed at how he shows himself and works in your heart. You're overwhelmed with joy because you learn more about his grace and patience toward you. He's saying, "I love being your Abba. Come; tell me everything. I'm here for you and will never leave you."

In child-like faith, crawl up in your Father's lap and be in his presence. Be honest and trust that he's listening—because you are his child and he is your Abba.

Prayer

Abba Father, you're a good and loving Father to me. Thank you for hearing my broken, feeble prayers that never feel enough. I know you hear me when I call out to you. Help me to be more natural with you so I can know you more. I love you. Amen.

DAY 28

Song of Redemption

"He has delivered us from the domain of
darkness and transferred us to the kingdom
of his beloved Son …"
Colossians 1:13

Recently, my husband and I had one of those out-of-the-ordinary evenings where we stayed up late in bed together chatting, reminiscing about our college and dating days, and expressing our gratefulness that God gave us one another when we least expected it. We reflected on our wedding day and all that led up to it.

"It's kind of sad … we never really had a song when we were dating," Jeremiah said.

I thought about it for a minute and it *was* kind of sad.

"We just chose one because we had to for our first dance," he added.

He was right. We dated for seven months and were engaged for six. Everything happened so fast. I thought about the beautiful song we chose (well, that he let me choose!), "When You Say You Love Me" by Josh Groban.

Our wedding day was just the beginning of our journey together. We weren't that "far" into it yet. Like our vows, we didn't fully understand the song lyrics or that a day might come when we'd be

It's to him you call for your rest, retreat, and rescue.

tempted to disband our sacred union. That there might be a day when our burning, unquenchable love wouldn't "always feel this way."

"I think the journey we've been on is our song," I told Jeremiah. "It tells the real story better than any mere love song could. Plus, our song is still being written."

Our almost 11 years of marriage have told a story of our sin exposed to the bone but also of unconditional love, acceptance, and grace—where we've seen our Savior's love shine brighter than the love we share. We know a Savior whose blood was shed for our freedom and righteousness. We worship a King who has rescued us out of darkness and brought us into light and who's restoring and making all things new.

Those of us who have trusted in Jesus all have a song of redemption, and it sings louder than all other love songs written by human, finite hands. Jesus Christ, God's Son, has reconciled us to himself—not because of anything we have done but because of everything he has done. We surrender to a Savior who cares deeply for our relationship so his song can be a pleasing melody for others to join in and be inspired by. So ultimately others can know what he is really like:

Patient. Forgiving. Sacrificial. Gentle. Kind. Humble. Faithful. Protective. Selfless. Strong. Truthful. Perfect. Sovereign. Unwavering. Unconditional. Enduring. Everlasting ...

This song of redemption—Christ's rescuing and restoring of broken people back to himself—is for you to behold personally. His salvation and deliverance changes everything. The overwhelming darkness you once aimlessly walked in is now a well-lit path guiding your feet to fullness of joy and restoration. It's to him you call for your rest, retreat, and rescue.

And that's something worth singing about.

Prayer

Father God, you're my redemption. Thank you that you make broken things beautiful; you have transferred me from the kingdom of darkness into your marvelous light. Continue to change me with your gospel. Amen.

DAY 29

Let Go and Follow

"And whoever does not take his cross and
follow me is not worthy of me."
Matthew 10:38

A few years ago I was given the opportunity to have
dinner with a bestselling author who was in town. Her
publisher wanted to treat both of us to a nice dinner at a
restaurant a half-hour away. I was excited for the opportunity
all week. It'd been snowy and icy all day, but I'd heard the
roads were manageable, so I thought I didn't have anything to
worry about.

Just a few minutes into driving on the interstate, the traffic was
backed up because of the ice. I was nervous but figured I was
already on the road and might as well stay put. Not only was I

scared to arrive at the icy ramps, but also my GPS didn't recognize the address of the restaurant. I called my husband and told him the whole situation. Then I broke down in tears.

"It's going to be okay, babe," he assured me.

I vented more of my frustrations and doubted his words. I was burning with anger at the circumstance.

"Why does the GPS have to do this to me? I'm going to be late, and I can't be late!" I yelled.

"I'm going to tell you where to go. Do you trust me?" He asked.

Ugh, I don't know.

Jeremiah was already on Google maps locating the road I was stuck on. I started to cool off and release control of what I couldn't manage in the first place. He navigated every road for me, and soon enough, I'd arrived at my destination. I was only a few minutes late and was even the first one there.

While I waited at our table, I texted: "You were right all along. I'm sorry for not trusting you—will you forgive me? I love you."

Just like in marriage when I struggle to let go, I have trouble releasing control in my relationship with the Lord because of fear. I'd rather grip the wheel and tell God, *I've got this. I can do this well! Let me find the way myself!* Even when I have no clue where I'm going and I'm scared of the dark.

Following God can be scary as we face the unknown. Once we've surrendered our will and our way to him, not knowing where he will take us can be unsettling and uncomfortable. The good news in Scripture is he tells us much of what his will already is. It's not always the grand mystery we often think.

In the Gospels, we see Matthew recounts the words of Jesus: "And whoever does not take his cross and follow me is not worthy of me."

Part of knowing the way as his follower is surrendering to him and taking up our cross daily. This is the only path that matters in life. It's a destination that cannot be found in a map coordinate but only in submission to Christ in the everyday experiences of our lives. Each of us has our own cross to bear: a difficult child, an illness, a broken marriage, an unexpected trial, a thorn in the flesh, scars from our past, or something that causes grief in our life.

The good news in Scripture is he tells us much of what his will already is

But it is often when we let go and follow what God would have us do, even in the pain, hurt, and suffering, he guides us and brings us to his will. And there will be joy at being counted as worthy by God, even in the most difficult of circumstances.

May we continually release control and let him lead.

Prayer

Jesus, sometimes the thought of giving my life to you and releasing control is terrifying. But I know that you're a good Father who knows me best and is directing my life. Help me to take up my cross daily and allow you to do as you please. You deserve all the glory, honor, and praise. Amen.

DAY 30

Little Light

"In the same way, let your light shine before
others, so that they may see your good
works and give glory to your Father who is
in heaven."
Matthew 5:16

I just feel like I'm not doing anything as a mom. I'm not
sure what my purpose is. I'm not really doing much," my
new friend said as we sipped on our lukewarm chai lattes. I felt
her pain. The dishes, laundry, messes, fits, disobedience, and
more sometimes make motherhood feel like it's just *not* worth
it. The common question remains: Why am I doing this, day in
and day out and for what benefit?

It's interesting how in many mom circles, we're trying to find our identity and purpose in the work we're doing. I'm all for moms doing what they love, having a business, or building a career if that's how they best serve their families. I'm a stay-at-home mom with a passion and calling to write, and I often feel the tension rising when my priorities are out of whack.

In the midst of all we have on our plates, we can't lose sight of our responsibility and mission to faithfully shepherd the hearts and lives of our children with the love of Jesus.

I'll never forget reading a book in my college child psychology class called *The Power of Mother Love*, which revealed the enormous impact a mother has upon her children from infancy, through the formative years, and into each developmental stage of their lives. The book marked me as a single woman years ago and still does today. When I get discouraged, I remember that book and that the work I'm doing isn't in vain even though at times it feels that way.

You're the hope of the world in the midst of the chaos and conflict in your home.

The impact we have upon our children as their very own Momma is massive. Like throwing a stone into deep water, the ripple effect of loving them reaches far and wide, into a future we may never one day see.

Jesus says that as Christ-followers, we're the light of the world. He doesn't say you "might" be the light of the world or you "will be someday," but you *are* the light. Right now, in your present circumstances, among the orange crushed goldfish on your clean floors, the piles of clothes scattered throughout your bedroom, and the dirty dishes overflowing in the sink.

You're the hope of the world in the midst of the chaos and conflict in your home. There's no plan B. To your children, home is wherever *you* are. Your primary mission field is in the home—where your husband and children are, where you long to be after a hard day's work or weeks of travel. Home—the place where love shines brightest into the hearts of your children. Home—where God sees your sacrifice and service as worthy.

This little light of mine, I'm gonna let it shine. Let it shine. Let it shine. Let it shine.

Prayer

Jesus, you've given me a vital and significant mission inside my home in loving the impressionable and moldable hearts of my children. I confess that it's the hardest work I've ever done. Give me the strength I need to shine my light brightly and to reach my children for your glory and honor. Amen.

LET YOUR *Light* shine BEFORE MEN IN SUCH A WAY THAT THEY MAY SEE YOUR *Good works,* & *Glorify your father* WHO IS IN HEAVEN.

MATTHEW 5:16

Extra Grace ...

30 Reasons You Might Be a Mom to Young Children ...

1. You find your morning cup of coffee still sitting in the microwave at 5:00 pm

2. The most popular comments in public are, "Wow, you have your hands full!" and "Are *all* those yours?"

3. You have 10 pacifiers and can't find any of them

4. Sitting in church service with your husband feels like a date

5. You no longer have to apologize to company for the house being a disaster

6. You can't remember the last time you had a full night's sleep

7. The only break you get is a potty break

8. Breaking up fights and disciplining is your job whether you like it or not

9. You won't dare go to the grocery store unless you're alone

10. Your third child doesn't mind eating off your second child's cold breakfast plate

11. You have to schedule your morning around how many dirty diapers need to be changed before going out

12. You consider lifting a 2 1/2 year old, 1 year old, and newborn as your weight-training class

13. You get annoyed that there aren't more mom-friendly, healthy drive-thru restaurants

14. You have to think twice whether or not you forgot a child

15. Visiting a good chiropractor is a nonnegotiable

16. You throw your kids at your husband as soon as he walks in the door

17. You pack all your kids in your van for a drive so you can have a conversation with your husband

18. Mother's Day Out, MOPS, and morning preschool are sanity savers

19. You've become good friends with your pediatrician

20. The only way to cook a meal is to put a kids show on

21. You are amazed you even got through another day

22. You're humbled because your son's teacher wrote you an encouraging email about your child, without knowing you've felt like a failure of a mom lately

23. You realize more than ever how precious life is and it's not a cliché; it's truly a gift

24. You want other people to experience the blessing of children, even when motherhood—no matter how many kids you have—is the hardest job ever

25. You're surprised that your capacity to love grows richer and deeper

26. You find yourself not wanting to ever miss out on each child's first milestone because you know how fast time has flown with the oldest

27. You pray every day that your children will come to know and love Jesus in spite of you

28. You ask God to do great things in and through your children so they can make a difference in the lives of others

29. You start to understand that the daily, difficult, messy, complicated, satisfying, beautiful, mundane tasks in raising your precious children are working together for a greater purpose—*When you serve them, you serve God*

30. It's a miracle you finished this book!

About the Author

Samantha Krieger is a pastor's wife, mother, and author. For more than 14 years, she has been writing for leading Christian magazines, books, websites, and devotionals.

Prior to becoming a stay-at-home mom, she wrote and edited Bible study curriculum for RightNow Media alongside the video teaching of pastors and authors including Max Lucado, Francis Chan, and Margaret Feinberg.

Currently, she is a regular contributor to FortheFamily.org and pens the column "Samantha's Salt" for her local newspaper. She is passionate about helping others live out their faith in real life.

Samantha attended Liberty University where she earned a B.A. in English and Liberty Theological Seminary, where she holds a Master of Arts in Religion. She and her husband Jeremiah live in Holyoke, Colorado, with their four children, John (8), Rebekah (6), Hannah (4), and Will (3).

Connect with Samantha
www.samanthakrieger.com
Twitter & Instagram: @samanthakrieger
Facebook: Samantha Krieger, Author